Chickadees in December

Bill O. Smith

illustrated by Charles R. Murphy

*For good tots everywhere,
especially you.*

At last.
Christmas is coming.

Busy busy elves
are working away
twenty-*five* hours a day.

But the Wheel-O-Matic is going wacky.

Half the duckies have no quacky.

A truck is stuck in the candy cane forest.

There's roaring new trouble in the Teddy Bear chorus.

And look at the top of the gingerbread shop.
The reindeer — the reindeer! — forgot how to stop.

Yes. It's a mess.

But you haven't heard the worst.
Beginning on December First,

there's a jolly someone,
I won't say who
(*but his favorite color isn't blue*).

He'll need a list.
He'll need it fast,
with every child's name,
first and last. Plus,
one final piece of information
vital to the North Pole nation:
    who remembered to be a good tot,
    and who forgot.

But time is short.
Who can he spare?
Who'd even dare
to travel thousands of miles
from city and farm
to lonely isles,
to find every boy and every girl
in every corner of the world
then turn around quick
and report back North
by December 24th…

Who?…

Reindeer!
No, they need more practice.

Elves?
No, too busy toy making.

Mrs. Claus??
Nope. Too busy baking.

Then *who?*...

...fee-b-bee, chick-a-dee...

Chick-a-dee!!

Of course.
Tough and tender, clever and bold,
never, ever afraid of the cold —

the chickadee —
swift of wing, heart of gold.

And so it is on December One,
millions of chickadees rise with the sun.
Tots!... are you ready?
The search has begun.

What's that…
…just out the window?
Are the chickadees already here?
If they're not here, they're very near.
I know some questions they have for you…

…shhh…

blink two times,
and I'll share a few.

Can you wiggle your toes?...
your nose?... maybe an ear?

Are you older
than you were last year?

Are you nice to others,
even the mean ones?

Do you eat your vegetables,
even some green ones?

Can you name a deer
that knows how to fly?

Is one of your favorite
questions "Why???"

Excellent.

Now,
one last question —
it's the best —
more important
than all the rest.

Close your eyes,
double tight…

long ago and far away,
what happened
on a
clear
calm
silent night?

And maybe you're not always perfectly good
and don't always act like you perfectly should,
but do you try?

Yes, a birthday…
…a birthday that changed the world!

Well done. You answered each question, every one.

Now the chickadees must hurry back North
to share the good news by...
when???

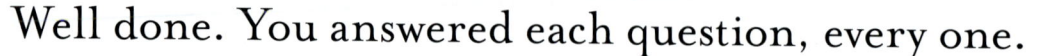

And look!
Wheels are spinning. Duckies are quacky.

The trouble is fixed. Teddies are happy.

And the reindeer even learned how to stop on that tricky slicky gingerbread shop.

Elves are humming, nutcrackers drumming.
Hallelujah!
Christmas is coming.

So for now,
little one,
take rest,
take rest.
You are loved. We are blessed.

Still,
tomorrow,
when you wake up,
you might make your bed,
or feed the pup.

It's always, always wise to remember —
chickadees in December.

**Chickadees have so many questions.
Here's a sampling of a few more:**

Do you always look both ways before crossing?
Are you brushing each day, and sometimes flossing?

Do you use words like "thank you" and "please"?
Do you love oceans, and mountains, and trees?

Do you do chores without a reminder?
We know you are kind, but could you be kinder?

Pretend you have wings, and live in a tree —
can you sing the song of a chickadee?

**If you have other questions, just for your tot,
write them here:**

_____

_____

_____

Text and Illustration Copyright © 2022 by Bill O. Smith
Design by Jenifer Thomas: www.drawbigdesign.com
First Edition
Published by Sleepytime Press
Printed in the USA
by Bang Printing, Brainard, Minnesota
Email: sleepytimepress@gmail.com
Website: www.billosmith.com
Library of Congress Control Number: 2021901055
ISBN: 978-0-9895238-4-4